Transforming School Climate Through Innovative Solutions

Transforming School Climate Through Innovative Solutions

A COLLABORATIVE LEARNING SOLUTIONS PUBLICATION

Edited by:

Christine Fonseca

Copyright © 2017 by Collaborative Learning Solutions.
Edited by Christine Fonseca
Cover Design by Steven Novak, Novak Illustration
Book Layout Design by Book Design Templates and Christine Fonseca

Transforming school climate through innovative solutions/edited by Christine Fonseca.
Includes bibliographical references.
ISBN-13: 978-1542408899 (pbk.)
ISBN-10: 154240889X (pbk)

Printed in the Unites States of America.

At the time of this book's publication, all facts and figures cited are the most current available. All telephone numbers, addressed, and Web site URLs are accurate and active. All publications, organizations, Web sites, and other resources exist as described in the book, and all have been verified. The authors and Collaborative Learning Solutions make no warranty or guarantee concerning the information and materials given out by organizations or content found at Web sites, and we are not responsible for any changes that occur after this book's publication. If you find an error, please contact Collaborative Learning Solutions.

Collaborative Learning Solutions
43426 Business Park Dr.
Temecula, CA 92590
888-267-6096
http://clsteam.net

Contents

CHAPTER 1

Introduction

Jon Eyler

Collaborative Learning Solutions (CLS) is committed to challenging the status quo in education and disrupting the predictable outcomes for marginalized youth. We intentionally disrupt antiquated thinking. We practice humility, recognizing that we don't always have the answers and committing to a process of lifelong learning. Most importantly we focus relentlessly on relationships with people. Since 2010 we have partnered with hundreds of schools, districts and regionalized education agencies across the nation to support efforts around Positive Behavior Interventions and Support (PBIS), Restorative Practices (RP), Social Emotional Learning (SEL), Mindfulness, Multi-tiered System of Support (MTSS), and specialized cognitive-based programs for students with a history of challenging behavior. In California, CLS is one of the largest single providers of innovative school climate solutions around behavioral health and social-emotional wellness.

Over the past three years, education agencies in California have drastically increased efforts to address social-emotional and behavior wellness. There are numerous drivers behind these efforts (i.e. legislation, policy, accountability changes), but the single most influential driver has been the Local Control Accountability Plan (LCAP). This requirement has combined fiscal flexibility, agency autonomy, community engagement, and growth oriented accountability into one plan. The LCAP has brought a more intentional focus and a brighter light to the critical elements of behavioral health and social-emotional wellness. In response, education agencies have been challenged to implement school climate solutions with limited expertise in behavioral health. Collaborative Learning Solutions has come alongside schools and districts to provide the expertise needed to effectively implement these school climate solutions. Our consulting team brings more than 150 years of experience in behavioral health and leadership to the partnership with each education agency. The team is composed of nationally acclaimed authors, attorneys, teachers, professors, and educational leaders who have been recognized as experts in their fields.

This book puts forth a collection of articles reflecting the professional experiences, passions, interests and expertise of several members of this team. The book is intended to not only challenge the thinking of educational practitioners, but to provide practical and actionable suggestions for improving the social and emotional wellness of youth AND adults.

As you digest these articles, it is our hope that you find balance between affirmation and agitation. Though we certainly want to acknowledge and affirm the great work of educational leaders, we also want to intentionally create dissonance. Through this uncomfortable disruption, the status quo is challenged and a new path to substantial change and progress in education is paved.

As you dive into the details of this book,
we invite you to walk with us—
challenge the status quo,
embrace discomfort,
relentlessly support youth.

CHAPTER 2

Engaging in Equity Beyond Disproportionality

Jon Eyler

"How will we know when we have great schools?
When race and class cease to be predictors of achievement' - Pedro Noguera"
(Deriman, 2010, slide 10)

The Intersection

Student: Did you just see that?
Me: What are you talking about?
Student: This bitch got me all fucked up.
Me: WHAT are you talking about?
Student: Did you NOT just see the way she looked at us?
Me: WHAT?!? – I have no idea what you are talking about?

Several years ago this simple yet raw interaction with a student marked a profound milestone in my personal equity journey. It was an exchange between a student (black, female, adolescent) and myself (white, male, adult) that unfolded as we walked into a local grocery store to buy items for our program – a specialized class designed to serve students with a history of challenging behaviors.

So, what was it about this interaction that etched this memory and created a marker in my equity journey? It defined an abrupt point at which our two worlds collided – a point at which two sets of lived experiences knocked heads in a shared social experience. I refer to this simply as an *intersection*, the point at which my limited set of racialized experiences collided with my student's peppered and riddled set of racialized experiences. Poignant because of the stark contrast in our perceptions, the experience provided another concrete example of the racial oblivion in which I lived for most of my adult life.

The intersection provides a glimpse as to the foundation of human experience, vulnerability, transparency and moral drive that frames equity work. Many conceptualize the work of equity and/or disproportionality around the notion of equilibrium. Too often I see educational leaders rush to a set of solutions anchored in "balancing the numbers." The students we serve deserve a foundation deeper than mere numbers and a commitment far beyond compliance. As an empowered participant in this system of education, my simple and non-abrasive act of maintaining the status quo is equal to a direct contribution to perpetuating racism and disparate outcomes. Knowing what I know today about systems of privilege, power, and protection, I morally cannot sign on to the agenda of status quo. Yes, the fight against the institutionalized embodiment of racism is risky. It threatens the very opportunities and protections I enjoy today. However, it's the right battle to fight for our youth.

Significant Disproportionality In California

States receiving IDEA Part B funds are required to (a) collect and examine data regarding disproportionality, (b) establish criteria for determining whether or not local education agencies (LEA) are significantly disproportionate based on race and ethnicity, (c) establish requirements for LEAs to revise policies, practices and procedures that may be contributing to disproportionate outcomes, and (d) require LEAs to reserve 15% of IDEA Part B funds to address significant disproportionality (Topical Brief, 2007).

For the 2016-2017 school year, a total of 31 districts in California were identified by the Department of Education as having significant disproportionality. Though the data points and criterion used for these determinations are tied to federal indicators specific to students with disabilities, I have found, in most districts, the same patterns to exist in the general population.

Of the districts recently identified, 55% were flagged in the area of discipline, meaning the LEAs had a disproportionate number of students with disabilities having more than 10 days of suspension. The large majority of these designations are due to the over-identification of black students with disabilities having more than 10 days of suspension. Though suspensions are often a narrow and limited indicator of exclusionary discipline practices, they do tend to reflect general discipline practices and patterns for incidents not resulting in a suspension.

It is important to note that 27% of districts identified as significantly disproportionate were found to be over-identifying students in the disability category of Emotional Disturbance, and 16% of the districts were disproportionate in the proportion of students served in highly restrictive placements (i.e. nonpublic or residential treatment facilities). In more cases than not, these highly restrictive placements are utilized primarily for students with a history of significant behavioral concerns.

This abbreviated landscape of significant disproportionality in California provides only a glimpse into the reality of equity challenges for students served in California's educational system. The summary reflects outcomes based on indicators pertaining to students with disabilities only. However, based on my experience working with more than 30 significantly disproportionate LEAs throughout the state, it is clear the patterns identified within the students with disabilities (SWD) subgroup mirror the outcomes for students without disabilities. For example, if a district is found significantly disproportionate for black students with disabilities having more than 10 days of suspension, the district almost always has a disproportionate representation of black students in overall discipline and discipline resulting in suspension. It's rare to discover that these patterns of disproportionality are different in both subgroups of students.

The importance of this cannot be overstated. Many district leaders see the issue of disproportionality as a special education only concern, an assumption that often proves inaccurate. The identification of significant disproportionality is an opportunity to evaluate policies, procedures, and practices for all students. The challenge of disproportionality is not resolved within the special education department; it's more effectively addressed through educational and/or student services.

Federal Policy Update

In December 2016, The United States Department of Education released new federal regulations around Significant Disproportionality. Below is a summary of the new regulations, which will become effective January 18, 2017. Though these new regulations take effect at the start of 2017, it's important to note that the California Department of Education (CDE) has not yet released official guidance on how these changes will be interpreted and implemented in California – stay tuned!

Summary of New Federal Regulations

A Standard Methodology

States will now be required to use a common methodology for making determinations of significant disproportionality within its districts. The regulations state the use of a risk ratio or alternative risk ratio with guidance to States on minimum cell size and n-size parameters. Though the methodology is standardized, States continue to hold discretion as to the thresholds and standards for "reasonable progress."

Author's Commentary - this revision will create greater consistency with how states define disproportionality, but it continues to leave great flexibility to states regarding thresholds and "reasonable progress." The previous regulations seemed to provide too much flexibility to the extent that some states set the boundaries so wide that no districts within the state were reported to have significant disproportionality. It will be important to pay attention to how states define "reasonable thresholds" and "progress", and these new regulations are implemented. These changes have the potential to increase the number of districts identified as significantly disproportionate. The figures below represents a summary of the estimated impact (utilizing current data for districts in California) according to the CDE and OSEP(Duncan-Becerril, 2016):

Current Regulations: 31 LEAs identified
New Regulations (CDE Estimates):   288 LEAs identified
New Regulations (OSEP Estimates): 638 LEAs identified

Emphasis on Discipline

The regulations place greater emphasis on the type of incident and disciplinary actions (including suspensions and expulsions) and provide examples of factors possibly contributing to disproportionality. These examples include lack of access to screenings and inappropriate use of disciplinary removals.

> *Author's Commentary* - many schools have adopted a set of removal strategies masked in the language of intervention (i.e. on campus suspensions are now re-coded and referred to as interventions in the "PBIS room" or the "Restorative Practices" room). The concept of providing short-term interventions is great; however, the removal from class as punishment is both troublesome and often ineffective, particularly in light of these new regulations. Districts can expect a greater emphasis on developing coherent systems of screening, intervening and monitoring student responsiveness around behavior and mental health.

Addressing Significant Disproportionality

The new regulations state that districts must address any policy, practice or procedure it identifies (through a root cause analysis process) as contributing to significant disproportionality. The regulations continue to require that LEAs set aside 15% of IDEA Part B funds (referred to as Coordinated Early Intervening Services (CEIS) funds) to address Significant Disproportionality; however, the use of these funds may now be used to serve children from age 3 through grade 12, with and without disabilities.

> *Author's Commentary* - this comes as a welcomed revision for many LEAs, particularly those addressing challenges around Least Restrictive Environment (LRE) and/or the over-identification of students qualifying under the category of Autism. Many districts throughout

California rely heavily on the use of non-public schools and residential treatment centers. The added flexibility in the new regulations will allow districts to allocate CEIS monies to the development of new programs for students with disabilities within the school district, thus minimizing the reliance on non-public schools and residential treatment centers. As of the publication of this article, the California Department of Education has not yet released official guidance that would allow districts to utilize CEIS funds as outlined in the new regulations. Districts currently developing CEIS plans should continue to follow current regulations until the CDE provides guidance on the use of CEIS funds under the new regulations.

Acknowledgement of Improvement

The new regulations now provide flexibility to States *not* to identify LEAs as Significantly Disproportionate even when they exceed the established risk ratio threshold. If a LEA demonstrates "reasonable progress" in lowering the applicable risk ratio in each of the two consecutive prior years, the State now has flexibility *not* to identify the LEA as significantly disproportionate.

Author's Commentary - it will be interesting to see where the thresholds around risk ratios and reasonable progress are established in each state. However, given the guidance on reasonable parameters for risk ratio calculations, I anticipate a steep increase in the number of districts identified as significantly disproportionate across the nation. In California, this compliments a more progressive accountability system that now utilizes a growth-oriented framework rather than rigid, performance-based criterion.

Current Efforts to Address Equity and Significant Disproportionality in California

Districts across the state take a variety of approaches to address both equity and significant disproportionality, including training opportunities, policy reform, and data analysis. These approaches can be helpful to address concerns, but have some limitations. Appropriate approaches that work to address the root causes of disproportionality are vital if districts are going to be more equitable.

Training into Equity

Over the past six years, I have experienced many districts responding to significant disproportionality through a strategy of professional learning. Training topics have included: white privilege, implicit or unconscious bias, critical race theory, disproportionality, stereotype threat, deficit thinking, and color-blindness. Though these efforts have gained much traction in recent years, my caution to leaders is to spend adequate time establishing a solid moral purpose and foundation for these learning opportunities.

I further suggest focusing first on building trust and vulnerability among the adults receiving the training. Much of these professional development offerings require participants to look inward, evaluate lived experiences, and consider perspectives and opinions that are often very different than their own. This requires a set of social and emotional competencies (i.e. self-reflection, vulnerability, trust, flexible thinking, social awareness) that may need to be developed prior to intensive equity training.

These professional learning strategies are great for beginning the work around equity and creating awareness. However, the most substantial impact on students is instructional practice in the classroom.

Focusing on building the capacity and self-efficacy of educational leaders to lead this work in schools and influence instructional practice is what directly impacts the lives of kids. See other articles in this publication for practical guidance related to building capacity and instructional practices.

The Practice Pointers below highlight important considerations for districts looking to initiate a training strategy around equity.

PRACTICE POINTERS: PROFESSIONAL DEVELOPMENT

➤ Define the framework to which the equity trainings connect. How do efforts to address equity work in tandem with district initiatives: MTSS, RTI, PBIS, Instruction, CTE, College and Career Readiness?

➤ Establish the moral foundation or the WHY that drives this work. A significant disproportionality designation from the CDE cannot and should not be the driver for focusing on equity in schools. What is the deeper WHY or moral driver for this work?

➤ Ensure a healthy foundation (i.e. social and emotional wellness among adults) in which to embed the equity work. Focus first on taking care of the adults in the organization. Some ideas include team building activities, mindfulness, compassion challenges, synergy days.

➤ Situate trainings around equity within an overarching set of equity goals for the district. Equity should not be another initiative; rather, it should appear in various aspects of the organization (human resources, fiscal allocations, student outcomes). Does your district have an equity vision or goals? Fergus (2016) suggests the following three components be evident in an equity vision: Numerical (name the outcome to be changed), Social Justice (name the access and opportunity to achieve or change), Culture/Belief (name and reduce the beliefs that frame and impact perceptions of cognitive and behavioral abilities).

Legislating Equitable Outcomes through Policy Revisions

Districts have taken bold actions to approve dramatic policy changes intended to restrict or prevent inequitable outcomes, particularly in the area of discipline. Though these efforts produce fairly immediate results in reducing risk, composition, or classification rates, they often fail to address the core root causes of disparate outcomes. More recently we have seen this in response to changing state legislation and policy priorities around student discipline. Many districts have restricted the use of in-school and out-of-school suspensions to some extent. These policy changes have resulted in drastic reductions in suspension rates across the state.

While these policy changes have had an immense impact on the surface, many professionals within the field would argue that they have failed to address the root causes of why students are (1) disproportionately sent out of the classroom and/or (2) disproportionately disciplined utilizing removal or reduction-oriented strategies.

The Practice Pointers on page 13 provide assistance for districts wanting to address the root causes of disproportionality.

Analyzing, Tracking, and Admiring Outcomes

Another common response to addressing equity is an intentional focus on disaggregating student outcome data (i.e. suspensions, discipline referrals), often including discipline outcome data in their accountability plans (i.e. LCAP). Though this is a great practice, the disaggregation of data alone does not change the root causes of disparate outcomes; it simply confirms the fact that the pattern still exists.

As districts embrace the technical aspects of illuminating disproportionality through the use of data and analytics, I suggest we pair this work with the adaptive aspects of leading equity. Heifetz,

---

PRACTICE POINTERS:
ROOT CAUSES

➤ Continue to monitor trends related to disproportionate suspension rates, but pay closer attention to patterns of office referrals, minor misbehavior, adult referrals for behavior/mental health interventions, and fidelity indicators around Positive Behavior Interventions and Supports (PBIS) and Restorative Practices (RP). Many schools focus solely on student outcome indicators (attendance, suspensions, referrals). Process or fidelity indicators are equally important in addressing the challenges associated with disproportionate representation.

➤ Revise progressive discipline guidelines to include flexibility for administrators to provide a response that meets the needs of the student. Having the discipline guide that dictates the same response for all students is not equitable. It assumes a motivational deficit behind the misbehavior, and it assumes that all students need the same response for correcting the behavior. A rigid discipline matrix restricts the ability of school administrators to utilize restorative and increase-oriented responses to student misbehavior.

➤ Also revise guidelines to reflect both reduction-oriented responses and increase-oriented responses. Increase-oriented responses to misbehavior are instructional and/or restorative in nature. They focus specifically on building a particular skill (empathy, compassion, self-regulation, flexible thinking). A prescriptive discipline policy does not allow the flexibility to provide students with what they need. The prescriptive "same response for all" approach inhibits equitable outcomes and restricts the likelihood that students get what they need to reduce further misbehavior.

Grashow & Linsky (2009) describe adaptive leadership as that which requires leaders to challenge people's familiar reality. It calls for shedding outdated approaches, embracing new skills and attitudes. It's threatening and dangerous, but necessary to guide organizations in the 21st century. The challenge to educational leaders today is to accompany the technical aspects of equity (analyzing, tracking student outcome data) with the adaptive aspects required to fully address equitable outcomes for students.

The Practice Pointers below provide guidance for districts in using data as part of a larger strategy around equity and disproportionality.

PRACTICE POINTERS: DATA

➢ Explore and become comfortable with talking about oneself as racial and cultural beings; this includes recognizing personal values, biases, and assumptions (Fergus, 2016)

➢ Utilize data to shape conversations about how bias-based beliefs contribute to the disparities. These may include the following: colorblindness, deficit thinking, unconscious bias, poverty-disciplining (Fergus, 2016).

➢ Develop a common protocol for how school site teams can act upon and respond to disparate student outcomes

➢ Involve students, parent, and community in developing action plans. These stakeholders offer perspectives that are often absent the problem-solving process. They provide great insights about what may be contributing to disproportionate outcomes.

A Charge to the Educational System

Knowledge of how systems create or hinder opportunity brings about a new level of responsibility for those working in the system. As a white, middle-class, male I carry the greatest set of protections and privileges in our school system and our society at large. Having this knowledge of how systems create or hinder opportunity, I also carry the greatest responsibility to push up against the status quo and question the system that has served me so well.

Some suggest this is risky, maybe even dangerous. Why should I be interested in disrupting a system in which I am the greatest benefactor? What drives my passion? His name is Dondre, DeShojn, Andrew, and Victor. Her name is Kamiesha, Ariel, Bethany, and Chauncey. It's my direct experience and involvement with kids that ignited my passion to challenge the status quo. Throughout most of California, I can predict the patterns and outcomes of students based on race, ethnicity, socio-economic status, and gender. I am now in a position to do something drastic to change this predictable trajectory for so many of our youth. The charge to you is to do the same – find discomfort in the status quo, take a risk, and disrupt education-as-usual!

The work around equity can best be described as a journey,
not a destination.
Embrace the journey.
Welcome the dissonance.
Find comfort in the productive struggle.
Be relentless!

References

Derminan, G. (2010). Pedagogy For All [PowerPoint slides]. Retrieved January 3, 2017 from http://www.slideshare.net/Malitaa1/pedagogy-for-all-aug-30-2010-supplemental-day.

Duncan-Becerril, S. (2016). A Time of Change [PowerPoint slides].

Fergus, E. (2016). Solving Disproportionality and Achieving Equity: A Leader's Guide to Using Data to Change Hearts and Minds. Thousand Oaks, CA: Corwin Press.

Heifetz, R. A., Linsky, M., & Grashow, A. (2009). The practice of adaptive leadership: Tools and tactics for changing your organization and the world. Cambridge, MA: Harvard Business Press.

Topical Brief: Disproportionatliy (2007). Retrieved December 29, 2016 from
    http://idea.ed.gov/explore/view/p/,root,dynamic,TopicalBrief,7, .

CHAPTER 3

Tier I Instruction: Including the "Other" in "All"

Micki Singer and Pauline Stahl

In a multi-tiered system of support, teachers are charged with the extremely challenging task of ensuring students thrive both academically and socially. All students must receive rich learning experiences "every year in every setting with every teacher, not merely in some years in some settings with some teachers" (Howard, 2009, p. 15). For students who are traditionally marginalized in society, those who are *other than* the norm, this can be elusive when their daily experience may include silence, alienation, and invisibility.

"Othering" Paley, N. (2010). CC-BY-SA Nina Paley

To fulfill the promise of Tier One Instruction for all, educators must transform their classrooms and curriculum to recognize their students' multi-dimensional, and sometimes fluid, identities.

Society creates narratives telling us what is "normal" (Foucault, 1990). These narratives manifest in virtually every aspect of society, including our schools. In the classroom, dominant discourses about race, gender, sexuality, sex, gender, and class shape the ways topics are discussed, resulting in some students feeling excluded or abnormal. These students become the "other" and often internalize their inferior status (Kumashiro, 2000). The *othered* view themselves as "objects" to whom life happens outside their control as opposed to being "subjects" in control of their destiny. Those who are *othered* in the classroom feel alienated and unable to fully participate in their education (Celoria, 2016).

Despite the mandate for critical thinking in Common Core, students are still too often required to be receptacles rather than constructors of knowledge. Our goal as educators should be to provide an environment where all students can gain a sense of agency, the capacity to act as a subject in the world from an honest sense of who they are. Only then will all students be able to fully participate in their own education.

Delivering curriculum that reinforces socially constructed narratives without question or opposition renders those narratives unalienable, denying educational entre for those who cannot see their experiences. In order for students to develop agency, they must feel safe to express their own experiences and understandings as well as challenge the dominant discourses they encounter in the curriculum. For example, depolarizing elements of identity, such as race or gender, would free students from being essentialized ("I am, and therefore I am not."), and allow expression of who they truly understand themselves to be (Anzaldúa, 2012). This type of democratic, student-centered learning incorporates and values the needs and realities of the individual. Regardless of content area, the Tier One classroom must be one where all students are able to see themselves and where sharing one's identity and reality is both expected and encouraged.

To fully participate in the construction of knowledge students need opportunities to learn about themselves in a positive light and incorporate their own life experiences with those of others. "If students are not able to transform their lived experiences into knowledge and to use the already acquired knowledge as a process to unveil new knowledge, they will never be able to participate rigorously in dialogue as a process of learning" (Macedo, 2000, p.19). Tier One classroom instruction must engender a positive environment where every student feels their experiences are valued and accepted, and one where questioning and challenging the curriculum is expected rather than allowed.

This type of classroom does not happen without intention and will require professional learning and collaboration to restructure classroom expectations as well as lesson conception and delivery. First, teachers must challenge their assumptions and beliefs about their own unconscious and/or unintended exclusionary practices. There are students in *every* classroom with experiences and forms of identity they do not feel they can freely express. Perpetuating only a single view or paradigm silences the "others." Next, teachers will need to explore curricula that encourage student questioning and personal expression, such as *Inquiry By Design* (2016), *Facing History* (2016), or *California Education and the Environment Initiative* (2016). An essential part of these curricula requires students to share their learning and experiences and challenge one another. Finally, teachers must encourage authentic dialogue by viewing all curricula, texts and research utilized in the classroom as generative rather than prescriptive. To do this, they will need collaborative opportunities to explore how to address the influence of dominant narratives "behind" the curriculum and ways to encourage the expression of counter narratives (Ladson-Billings & Tate, 1995).

The benefits of truly inclusive Tier One classroom instruction far outweigh the investment, especially for our most at-risk students. Encouraging students to challenge what they learn, and express their lived experiences in an accepting environment will help all students develop a sense of agency in their lives. Creating a positive, accepting classroom environment that encourages multiple viewpoints allows students to express their current understandings while grappling with new knowledge. It gives voice to the voiceless, counters oppression, and results in a more democratic education for *all* students (Freire, 2000).

References

Anzaldúa, G. (2012). *Borderlands: The new mestizo = La Frontera*. San Francisco, CA: Aunt Lute Books.

California Education and the Environment Initiative. (2016). Retrieved December 4, 2016 from www.californiaeei.org/

Celoria, D. (2016). The Preparation of Inclusive Social Justice Education Leaders. *Educational Leadership and Administration, 27*, 199.

Facing History and Ourselves. (n.d.) Retrieved December 4, 2016 from https://www.facinghistory.org/

Foucault, M. (1990). *The history of sexuality: An introduction* (R. Hurley, Trans.). NewYork, NY: Vintage Books.

Freire, P. (2000). *Pedagogy of the oppressed: 30th anniversary edition*. New York, NY: Continuum.

Howard, M. (2009). *MISS from all sides: What every teacher needs to know*. Portsmouth, NH: Heinemann.

Inquiry By Design. (n.d.) Retrieved December 4, 2016 from http://inquirybydesign.com

Kumashiro, K. (2000). Toward a theory of anti-oppressive education. *Review of Educational Research, 70*(1), 25-53.

Ladson-Billings, G., & Tate, W. (1995). Toward a critical race theory of education. *Teachers College Record, 97*(1), 47.

Macedo, D. (2000). Introduction. In P. Freire, *Pedagogy of the Oppressed* (30th anniversary ed, pp. 11-27). New York, NY: Continuum.

Paley, N. (2010). Othering [Digital image]. Retrieved December 1, 2016, from http://mimiandeunice.com/2010/07/29/othering/

CHAPTER 4

Necessary Components to Ensure Initiative Sustainability

Gail Angus

Over the years, schools and districts throughout the nation have implemented numerous initiatives and programs to support student learning and engagement. Some of these implementations have resulted in a high degree of positive outcomes only to have initiative disappear within a short period of time. Why do some initiatives go away even after experiencing a positive impact?

Whenever a school or district team decides to implement a new initiative, they are excited, passionate and determined to do their best. They believe the new program will make a difference. Everyone engages the work thinking this time it will be different; all the effort and work will be worth doing, and the initiative will be sustainable. If you are part of a team leading the work with initiatives such as MTSS, PBIS, RtI, equity, or other school climate ideas, you may have experienced these thoughts. You may have structured goals around both successful implementation and sustainability.

Successful implementation of any initiative requires a site leadership team, administrative support, and coaching (Ervin, 2007; Simenson, 2003; Sugai & Horner, 2002). Development of an action plan that describes on-going training, a process for periodic evalua-tion of the initiative (Barret et al., 2008), review and revision of poli-cies, and securing funding to support the work (Sugai & Horner, 2004) is also part of a strong implementation plan.

Sustainability requires similar components, including site-level administrative support, a team approach to implementation, staff commitment and technical assistance. District-level support, includ-ing a data management process, funding and policies and procedures that are in alignment with the initiative are also necessary (Bambara et al., 2012; Coffey & Horner, 2012; Mathews et al., 2014; McIntosh et al., 2016; Mercer et al., 2014; Pinkelman et al., 2015; and Turri et al., 2016).

Site Level Components

Administrator Support:
Numerous studies have examined the key strategies that serve to support or hinder the implementation of educational initiatives. Site administrative support is consistently highlighted as a key component responsible for both the success and failure of an initiative (Bambara, et. al., 2012; Coffey & Horner, 2012; Mathews, et. al., 2014; McIn-tosh, et. al., 2016; Mercer, et. al., 2014; Pinkelman, et. al., 2015; and Turri, et. al., 2016). Further analysis of the research indicates that an administrator's attitude and public support is crucial to success (Bambara, et. al., 2012; Coffey & Horner, 2012; Mathews, et. al., 2014; McIntosh, et. al., 2016; Mercer, et. al., 2014; Pinkelman, et. al., 2015; and Turri, et. al., 2016). In fact, when those components are missing, lack of administrative support is identified as the largest bar-rier to implementation (Pinkelman, et.al., 2015). Participation in site-level implementation meetings, initiative inclusion in staff-wide meet-ings, providing ample time for team members to work on necessary

implementation structures, and allocation of resources (human and material) are all ways administrators can demonstrate support for an initiative (Bambara, et. al., 2012).

Sometimes site administrators struggle with commitment toward a specific initiative. When asked what were the barriers to their support, site administrators cite a lack of understanding or skill around the initiative, conflicts between the initiative goals and personal or philosophical beliefs, unsupportive staff, or unrealistic district-level goals for implementation (McIntosh, et. al., 2016). These same site-level administrators shifted their attitude regarding the work when provided with opportunities to learn more about the initiative through informational trainings, networked with sites that had experienced successful implementation of similar initiative, and worked with other administrators around the initiative (McIntosh, et. al., 2016).

Staff Commitment:

Research highlights staff commitment as another important component of implementation and sustainability (Sugai & Horner, 2006). Administrators agree, pointing to staff support as a critical factor in their willingness and desire to lead the work (McIntosh, et. al., 2016). Staff commitment is cultivated through the following steps:

> Train staff regarding the "why" behind the initiative (Coffey & Horner, 2012)
> Provide the tools and skills necessary to implement the initiative (Mathews, et. al., 2014)
> Develop opportunities for success and models of successful implementation (McIntosh, et. al., 2016)
> Establish and maintain priority status of the initiative through administrative support and site goals (Pinkelman, et.al., 2015)

Technical Assistance:

On-going training and coaching through the implementation phase are necessary for sustainability (Ervin, 2007; Sugai & Horner, 2004; Simenson, 2003; and Sugai & Horner, 2002). Many teams receive modest professional development and are left to implement the initiative on their own. However, without ongoing technical assistance many sites experience difficulties with the actual implementation of the initiative (Sugai & Horner 2004). On-going coaching provides accountability and ensures the acquisition by teams of the necessary skills to lead, build and support the work (Mathews, et. al., 2014). Additional strategies to support the training of new staff will aid sustainability.

Data:

The development of a protocol for data collection and analysis is necessary for both the initial implementation process and sustainability of the initiative (Coffey & Horner, 2012; Mathews, et. al. 2014). The information gathered from the data, including fidelity and outcome measures, supports regeneration (Coffey & Horner, 2012). It enables a team to troubleshoot possible barriers to implementation, be responsive to student and staff needs and highlight successes.

District Level Support

Current research identifies district support as a required element of initiative sustainability (Coffey & Horner, 2012). This has lead to organizations like the Michigan Integrated Behavior and Learning Support Initiative refusing to work with districts unless the superintendent, all assistant superintendents and other key district and site level administrators commit to supporting the implementation of the initiative for 3-5 years (Goodman, 2016). Without that

---

Initiative Sustainability Checklist – District Level

☐ District Administration is trained and understands the initiative

☐ District is committed to the initiative, as demonstrated through district goals

☐ Policies and procedures are in place to support the initiative

☐ Funding is secured for 5 years to support the initiative

☐ District has established monthly/quarterly meeting to support ongoing learning and sharing of skills

☐ Data system is in place for collecting data and synthesizing the information into a useable format

☐ Data is provided at least monthly to schools for review

☐ District personnel has visited other districts and/or sites who have implemented the initiative

---

commitment, any district leader at any time can create a barrier to implementation or sustainability efforts by creating competitive initiatives or removing funding (Goodman, 2016; Mercer, et. al., 2014; Pinkelman, et. al., 2015).

In addition to the involvement and commitment of key personnel, districts can support sustaining initiatives by developing policies and procedures in alignment with the work (Sugai & Horner, 2004). Also, funding the initiative through the district budget for 3-5 years enables the availability of resources, human and material, necessary to move the work forward (Pinkelman, et.al., 2015; Sugai & Horner, 2004; and Turri, et. al., 2016). Finally, creating a system of data collection that allows ease of analysis by the sites supports the use of data for decision-making and problem solving (Coffey & Horner, 2012; Pinkelman, et. al., 2015)

Initiative Sustainability Checklist - Site Level

☐ Site Administration is trained and understands the initiative

☐ Site Administration is committed to the initiative, as demonstrated through site goals

☐ Networking - site administrator and team network with other teams implementing similar initiatives

☐ Site participates in district or regionally provided meetings to support on-going learning and sharing of skills

☐ Sites visit other schools implementing the initiative

☐ Site administrator and staff understand why the initiative is being implemented

☐ Staff has been trained

☐ A strategy has been developed for sharing the experience of the initiative with others

☐ Site administrator talks and models the initiative often (e.g. on staff agenda, mentioned during assemblies and daily announcements)

☐ Time is provided during the school day to work on developing the initiative

☐ Structures for supporting the initiative are integrated into the school environment and schedule

☐ Data is provided and reviewed at least monthly for problem-solving

☐ Technical assistance, on-going coaching, and training is secured

☐ A strategy is developed for training new staff on the initiative

The district sustainability checklist on page 27 and the site sustainability checklist above provide a quick way to ensure the presence and consideration of sustainability items. This guide can be used by district or site teams to assist with implementation. Any program or initiative can be sustained when time and energy is intentionally given to these necessary components.

References

Bambara, L. M., Goh, A., Kern, L., & Caskie, G., (2012). Preceived barriers and enablers to implementing indivualized positive behavior interventions and supports in school settings. *Journal of Positive Behavior Interventions*, 14(4), 228–240. DOI: 10.1177/1098300712437219

Barrett, S. B., Bradshaw, C. P., & Lewis-Palmer, T. (2008). Maryland statewide PBIS initiative: Systems, evaluation, and next steps. *Journal of Positive Behavior Interventions, 10(2)*, 105-114. DOI:10.1177/1098300707312541

Coffey, J. H., & Horner, R. H., (2012). The sustainabilitity of schoolwide positive behavior interventions and supports. *Council for Exceptional Children, 78(4)*, 407-422.

Ervin, R. A., Schaughency, E., Matthews, A., Goodman, S. D., & McGlinchey, M. T. (2007). Primary and secondary prevention of behavior difficulties: Developing a data-informed problem-solving model to guide decision making at a school-wide level. *Psychology in the Schools, 44(1)*, 7-18. DOI:10.1002/pits.20201

Goodman, S. (Presenter). (August 31, 2016). District level adoption of MTSS: The engine to drive sustainable change. [Webinar series]. Michigan: Association of Positive Behavior Support.

Mathews, S., NcIntosh, K., Frank, J. L., & May, S. L., (2014). Critical features predicting sustained implementation of school-wide positive behavioral interventions and supports. Journal of Positive Behavior Interventions, 16(3), 168–178. DOI: 10.1177/1098300713484065

McIntosh, K., Kelm, J. L., & Canizal Delabra, A. (2016). In search of how principals change: Events that help and hinder administrator support for school-wide positive behavioral interventions and supports. Journal of Positive Behavior Interventions, 18, 100-110.

Mercer, S. H., McIntosh, K., & Strickland-Cohen, K., (2014). Measurement invariance of an instrument assessing sustainability of school-based universal behavior practices. School Psychology Quarterly, 29(2), 125-137. DOI: 10.1037/spq0000054

Pinkelman, S. E., McIntosh, K., Rasplica, C. K., Berg, T., & Strickland-Cohen, K., (2015). Perceived enablers and barriers related to sustainability of school–wide positive behavioral interventions and supports. Behavioral Disorders, 40(3), 171-183.

Simonsen, B., Sugai, G., & Fairbanks, S. (2007). School-wide positive behavior support: Preventing the development and occurrence of problem behavior. In S. W. Evans, M. D. Weist, & Z. N. Sempell, *Advances in school –based mental health interventions: Best practices and program models*, V. II (pp. 8.1-8.17). Kingston, N.J.: Civic Research Institute.

Sugai, G., & Horner, R. (2002). The evolution of discipline practices: School-wide positive behavior supports. *Child & Family Behavior Therapy*, 24(1-2), 23-50. DOI:10.1300/J019v24n01_03

Sugai, G., & Horner, R. H. (2004). School-wide positive behavior support: Implementer's blueprint and self-assessment. Retrieved on January 16, 2010, from OSEP Technical Assistance Center on Positive Behavioral Interventions and Supports.
http://www.pbis.org/pbis_resource_detail_page.aspx?Type=3&PBIS_ResourceID=284

Sugai, G., & Horner, R. H. (2006). A promising approach for expanding and sustaining school-wide positive behavior support. *School Psychology Review, 35*(2), 245-259.
http://www.nasponline.org/publications/spr/index.aspx?vol=35&issue=2

Turri, M. G., Mercer, S. H., McIntosh, K. Nese, R. N. T., Strickland-Cohen, & Hoselton, R., (2016). Examining barriers to sustained implementation of school-wide prevention practices. *Assessment for Effective Intervention*, Vol. 42(1) 6–17. DOI: 10.1177/1534508416634624

Five Reasons Why Building Capacity Is Critical for Educational Leaders

Mary Beth Kropp

Words are funny things. They are full of meaning and make our world more vibrant and exciting, yet I often don't take the time to realize their full value. Capacity is one of those words. I did not understand it's full meaning until I realized how difficult it was to work without it. The Oxford Press defines the noun *capacity* in three ways: "the amount something can hold; the ability or power to do, experience, or understand something; and a specified role or position," (Oxford Press, 2016). As a leader, I have found my best work combined all of these elements as I worked with teachers, students, and families in robust and productive teams.

Capacity stems from the Latin word *capere*, meaning to take or hold. For school leaders, capacity building is one of the most important aspects of our position. Our ultimate goal as educators is to help students define their abilities and realize their full potential as they become contributing members of society. This is no simple task. Focusing on the development of human capital, the roles of teachers, parents, and students, however, has made the work easier and more fulfilling. As I have capitalized on the collective strengths of the brilliant minds I have worked with as a principal, I have increased my individual leadership abilities and positively influenced the aptitude of the team, resulting in opportunities to deepen student impact.

Cultivating capacity is the linchpin to team success. Consider these five evidence-based reasons:

- ❖ Creates Collaboration and Connections
- ❖ Ignites Innovation and Creativity
- ❖ Engages and Empowers Staff
- ❖ Facilitates Fun and Happiness
- ❖ Capacity Strengthens Sustainability

Collaboration and Connections

The collaborative effect produces greater perspective and 'buy in' when teams are faced with change. Working on a productive team creates a synergy that is far more powerful than one could ever muster up as an individual. When the climate is positive and supportive, and the team feels that they are contributing to the greater good and are more willing to bring different perspectives and ideas to the table, collaboration will create infinite possibilities.

Team members are more likely to embrace change when they have a voice in addressing and implementing it. Research in professional learning communities has shown that working in a team not only breaks down the silos often created in schools but leads to higher production and the response to students' specific needs (DuFour & DuFour, 2007, Fullan 2008).

A Culture of Innovation

When teams get together for the sole purpose of reflecting on what is and what could be, the gate to innovation is burst wide open! Leaders must create the culture of innovation at schools, and when they do, both faculty and students win. Staff members have unique strengths, and when we bring those together, we create the opportunity for multi-dimensional learning. Taking a lesson from the business world, companies that foster teamwork generate the greatest success (Catmull & Wallace, 2014; Dyer et al., 2011; Fay et al., 2015).

Everyone brings different ideas to our jobs based on our personal experiences, so when teams have the opportunity to share experiences as a way of discovering what could be, we foster the right environment to create something even more meaningful for our students. I have found that what teachers produce leads directly to what is implemented in the classroom. Finding time for staff members to work together not only builds individual teacher skills, but also provides a forum for a staff to build on their collective skills, enhancing the collective environment.

Engage and Empower

Hargraves and Fullan (2012, pg 8.) use the phrase "the power over vs. the power with" in their book, *Professional Capital: Transforming Teaching in Every School*. It speaks to the value of building capacity. Site leaders must capture the benefits of working *with* teams of teachers.

The influence teams create when they are empowered to make decisions together, try new strategies, and shape their school culture, widens the range of their impact. This helps catapult ideas forward with less resistance. Great leaders understand that engaging others builds real connections and real learning. Capacity for knowledge grows when team members are allowed to lead, engage, debate, and question each other (Rice, Marlow, & Masarech, 2012). When all of these things occur, trust increases, as does our capacity for learning.

Facilitating Fun and Happiness

Even Kid President understands the value of a team. In his bestselling book, *Kid President's Guide to Being Awesome*, 11-year old Kid President (a.k.a. Robby Novak) shares that teaming up with people makes any task more enjoyable. When *fun* is infused into group work, the team tends to gain more meaning from their time together. Enjoyable collaboration by teams leads to sustainable energy and enthusiasm for projects and meetings. When leaders foster a good laugh, they create opportunities for team members to relax and break down barriers they may have with each other.

Building in time for teams to add in a few happy diversions can facilitate positive relationships and connections amongst team members. Working in teams can also lead to great joy. Joy and happiness, in turn, develop both IQ and EQ. Daniel Goleman, the leader in the field of emotional intelligence, believes that group intelligence (IQ) is influenced by the group's collective emotional intelligence (EQ). Groups with high IQ often do better when their teams experience joy and harmony (Goleman, 1994).

Another benefit to laughter during periods of collaboration—space. A quick icebreaker or an opportunity to laugh while collaborating can help a team create 'space' that may be needed when the time comes for difficult conversations or important decisions. This is particularly important as teams begin the work on initiatives around equity, behavior or innovation.

Capacity Strengthens Sustainability.

When leaders support, encourage, and trust their teams, members often become leaders. Often, when team members commit to learning together, they tend to want to stay working together, with or without an administrator. In a school setting, it is impossible for the principal to continuously take the role of *trailblazer*. When teacher leaders are developed, nourished, and sustained, the capacity for success is increased dramatically (Lieberman & Friedrich, 2010) as they take on more leadership roles throughout the campus. When the workload is more balanced, we decrease the likelihood of burnout and the dreaded 'initiative fatigue' that so often spreads throughout schools.

How often have you heard the phrase "Together, Everyone Achieves More?" The simplicity of this phrase serves as a simple reminder—together, we *can* achieve more. When leaders understand that working in a team produces quicker and more meaningful results, everyone wins (Maxwell, 2002). Teams that are developed with a positive purpose foster an environment where it is safe to check your ego at the door. This allows team members to roll up their sleeves and focus on the tasks at hand. It is collective energy that produces great results.

One of the greatest benefits of deep capacity at a school site is the gift of time that allows leaders to develop other aspects of the school, including community and parent partnerships, working with a specific child, a mental break, or mentoring another colleague. The pace of the principalship can lead to increased stress and burnout, so it becomes imperative that leaders find ways to take time for themselves.

Consider the definition of *capacity* once again "the amount something can hold; the ability or power to do, experience, or understand something; and a specified role or position" (Oxford Press, 2016). By building capacity, school leaders influence an entire community.

As a principal, my role was defined through my job description and it was clear what I was expected to accomplish, yet the overwhelming scope of my work helped me realized just exactly what I could not complete on my own. As I worked with teams of staff, parents and students, not only did I find more joy and satisfaction with the work, I benefitted from our collective capacity to do, experience, and understand the needs of our students. School administrators have monumental jobs, but when we build our capacity with staff, parents, and students, we have opportunities to use our synergistic relationships to accomplish great things. It is then we can take the very best from all of us and hold each other accountable for our vision for student success.

References

Building a thriving work culture: focus on team and fun are among the top 5 tips. (2015, January). *Healthcare Registration*, 24(4), p. 9.

Catmull, E. E., & Wallace, A. (2014). Creativity, inc.: Overcoming the unseen forces that stand in the way of true inspiration (First ed.). New York, NY: Random House.

DuFour, R., & DuFour, B. (2007). What might be: Open the door to a better future. *Journal of Staff Development*, pgs. 28(3), 27-28, 70.

Dyer, J., Gregersen, H. B., 1958, & Christensen, C. M. (2011). *The innovator's DNA: Mastering the five skills of disruptive innovators*. Boston, MA: Harvard Business Press.

Fay, D., Shipton, H., West, M. A., & Patterson, M. (2015). Teamwork and organizational innovation: The moderating role of the HRM context. *Creativity and Innovation Management*, 24(2), pgs. 261-277.

Fullan, M. (2008). The six secrets of change: What the best leaders do to help their organizations survive and thrive (1st ed.). San Francisco, CA: Jossey-Bass.

Goleman, D. (1995). Emotional intelligence: Why it can matter more than IQ. New York, NY: Bantam.

Hargreaves, A., & Fullan, M. (2012). *Professional capital: Transforming teaching in every school*. New York, NY: Teachers College Press. Pgs. 8-9.

Lieberman, A., & Friedrich, L. (2010). *How teachers become leaders: learning from practice and research*. New York, NY: Teachers College Press.

Maxwell, J. C. (2006). The 17 essential qualities of a team player: Becoming the kind of person every team wants. Nashville, TN: Thomas Nelson Inc.

Montague, B., & Novak, R. (2015). Kid president's guide to being awesome. New York, NY: Harper Collins.

Oxford University Press. (2016). Oxford English dictionary. Oxford, England: Oxford University Press. Retrieved on December 30, 2016 from https://en.oxforddictionaries.com/definition/capacity.

Rice, C., Marlow, F., & Masarech, M. (2012). *The engagement equation*. Hoboken, NJ. Wiley & Sons, Inc.

Superville, D. R. (2014). Study finds principal mobility takes toll on budgets, learning. Education Week. Retrieved on December 31, 2016 from http://www.edweek.org/ew/articles/2014/11/12/12report-b1.h34.html

Creating a Climate of Calm and Compassion on Campus: Three Steps for Decreasing Staff Stress and Boosting Social Emotional Wellness

Joelle Hood

Worried about catching a cold from a colleague? What about catching stress? According to research, stress is contagious. In fact, a recent study revealed that the more stress a teacher experienced, the more cortisol (a.k.a. "the stress hormone") in his or her students' saliva (Oberle & Schonert-Reichl, 2016). Research not only documents the contagious nature of stress, it highlights its negative impact as an issue of global concern in the field of education (American Federation of Teachers, 2015; Davidson, 2011; Gallup, 2013; McCarthy et al., 2009; Skaalvik & Skaalvik, 2015; Stevenson & Harper, 2006).

Workplace stress can cause teachers to suffer physical symptoms like high blood pressure, insomnia, and fatigue, as well as psychological symptoms like anxiety, depression, and burnout (American Federation of Teachers, 2015; Skaalvik & Skaalvik, 2015; Teachers Assurance Report, 2013). Stress also has a profound impact on a teacher's professional performance. Teachers report that stress has caused their teaching to be below par. Additionally, the negative impact on student learning, including increased teacher absenteeism and turnover, decreased efficacy of instruction and diminished positive relationships with students and colleagues is well documented (Stevenson & Harper, 2006; Davidson, 2011; Green, 2014; Hydon et al., 2015; Teachers Assurance Report, 2013; Yu et al., 2015). It is likely these consequences also increase stress among site and district administrators. Teacher stress affects not only their individual social-emotional health but the well-being of the entire organization (Cartwright & Cooper, 2009).

Educational leaders and organizations have a responsibility to promote the health and wellness of their teachers (Stevenson & Harper, 2006). If we want our youth to grow up and become positive and productive citizens, then we must invest in our teachers and build their capacity to be the best possible versions of themselves every day! Promoting teacher health and wellness may seem like an insurmountable task, but it isn't. Here are three key areas that you can focus on to lower teacher stress, increase Social Emotional Wellness, and boost school climate at the same time:

✓ Strengthen School Climate with SEL
✓ Create Connections with Community Circles
✓ Make More Mindful Moments

STRENGTHEN SCHOOL CLIMATE WITH SEL

"The best climate for learning comes when students, teachers, and school leaders each take steps to become more emotionally self-aware and socially intelligent."

- Daniel Goleman, The Socially Intelligent Leader (Goleman, 2006, para. 5)

Teachers that have been trained and supported in implementing Social Emotional Learning (SEL) have lower job-related anxiety and depression, improved relationships and rapport with students, increased teacher engagement, and greater perceived control in their work (Abry et al., 2013). In fact, a newly released research report stated that developing SEL skills in adults improves professional interactions inside the school and prepares teachers to help students develop their SEL skills (Kendziora & Yoder, 2016).

Active SEL practices demonstrated by teachers are negatively associated with burnout (Ransford et al., 2009), and positively associated with job satisfaction (Brackett et al., 2010). Additionally, teachers implementing MTSS and/or PBIS report lower levels of job-related stress (Ross et al., 2012). The strategies below are designed to strengthen the implementation of SEL within the district, site, or classroom.

STRENGTHEN SCHOOL CLIMATE WITH SEL: THE STRATEGIES

✓ Create School Board and District policies and structures around SEL Implementation to provide the fiscal and personnel resources necessary to ensure sustainability.

✓ Align SEL Standards with Common Core Standards as well as Best Practices in Instructional Strategies for both SEL and Common Core so that teachers understand that these two areas aren't separate goals, but rather a stronger foundation together for supporting the education of the whole child and achieving academic success.

✓ Provide in-depth Professional Learning tied with Coaching to help strengthen SEL competencies in adults on campus, resulting in their lowered stress and improved SEL implementation for students.

CREATE CONNECTIONS WITH COMMUNITY CIRCLES

"Whenever possible, create a circle where people can safely share deep experiences and diverse viewpoints. There are many circle formats, but their one central concept is to demonstrate reverence for the truth of another person's experience."

- James O' Dea, Cultivating Peace ("Quotes – Empathy Circles", n.d., para.1)

According to Datnow (2011), a collaborative culture happens when teachers perceive collaboration to be valuable, productive, and pleasant, while contrived collegiality results from administrative regulations obliging teachers to collaborate. A teacher community, however, which extends deeper than collegiality and collaboration, is described as a group of teachers who are socially interdependent, participate together in discussion and decision making, and share and build knowledge with a group identity (Brouwer et al., 2012). Deep level teacher collaboration and community-building often occurs less frequently in schools. Opportunities for teachers to work with colleagues is typically restricted to more practical matters: lesson planning, testing, and discussions around the pace and content of the curriculum (Cheng & Ko, 2009; Plauborg, 2009; Visscher & Witziers, 2004).

Community Circles create an opportunity for school staff to build stronger social connections, a vital key to strengthening the immune system and improving overall health (Pressman et al., 2005), as well as decreasing levels of anxiety and depression (Lee et al., 2001). One research study even showed that spending time in positive social interactions with co-workers can lower blood pressure and decrease heart rate (Heaphy & Dutton, 2008).

On the flip side, research has shown that a lack of social connection is one of the greatest detriments to total health, delivering negative outcomes greater than obesity, smoking and high blood pressure

(House et al., 1988). Researchers found that when colleagues have an opportunity to talk about non-work related topics, communal bonding increases and stress levels decrease (Ozaki et al., 2012). Additionally, individuals who feel connected to others have higher self-esteem, greater empathy for others, and demonstrate more trust and cooperation (Lee et al., 2001).

Who wouldn't want a school staff rich in pro-social behaviors and overall health? Utilizing community circles to strengthen a sense of social connection creates a positive feedback loop of Social Emotional Wellness.

The strategies below focus on actively building community on your site or in your classrooms.

CREATE CONNECTIONS WITH COMMUNITY CIRCLES:
THE STRATEGIES

✓ Hold Department Meetings and Staff Meetings in circles, and start off meetings with discussion rounds to help staff get to know each other better and strengthen social connections.

✓ Create an advisory or homeroom period to give teachers an opportunity to hold community circles in the classroom.

✓ Provide Professional Learning workshops to provide teachers with the opportunity to experience being a participant in circles as well as learning strategies and tools to facilitate circles in the classroom or in meetings with colleagues.

MAKE OPPORTUNITES FOR MORE MINDFUL MOMENTS

"Between stimulus and response, there is a space. In that space lies our freedom and power to choose our response.
In our response, lies our growth and freedom."

-Viktor Frankl, Man's Search for Meaning ("Viktor E. Frankl", n.d., para. 1)

Professional development in mindfulness is gaining recent popularity in both corporate and educational settings. Corporate institutions such as Aetna, Google, Target, General Mills, Facebook, Eileen Fisher, and Ford Motor Company provide mindfulness training, resources, and support to employees (Gelles, 2015; Hunter, 2013) as part of their proactive focus on employee wellness. Kabat-Zinn (2003, p. 144) describes mindfulness as the "awareness that emerges from paying attention on purpose, in the present moment, and non-judgmentally to the unfolding of experience moment by moment." Research continues to emerge documenting the many benefits of mindfulness-based interventions (MBI) and training, including a strengthened ability to cope with difficult challenges, lowered stress levels, increased levels of self-compassion, improved ability to focus, and a greater sense of overall well-being (Byron et al., 2014; Erogul et al., 2014; Fries, 2009; Morledge et al., 2013).

Schools have begun to offer training in mindfulness for teachers to address stress (Flook et al., 2013; Flook et al., 2015). Mindfulness programs in schools have been shown to foster teachers' ability to focus awareness on the present moment in a responsive, non-reactive way, strengthening their capacity to relate to themselves and others in a more kind and patient manner (Bishop et al., 2004). Mindfulness training programs for teachers resulted in decreased stress, anxiety, and burnout and increased empathy, forgiveness, and personal growth (Jennings et al., 2013). A 2015 mixed-methods study (Taylor et al., 2015) revealed that emotion regulation and pro-social tendencies like compassion and forgiveness changed as a function of the mindfulness intervention and helped to reduce stress. Participants also developed greater efficacy in meeting emotional demands in the classroom and showed less negative emotional reactions to stressors at work.

Practical ideas for incorporating mindfulness onto your site and in the classroom are indicated below. These activities will cultivate opportunities to practice awareness and increase social-emotional competencies.

OPPORTUNITIES FOR MINDFUL MOMENTS: THE STRATEGIES

✓ Provide Professional Learning workshops on Mindfulness for Educators and Mindfulness for Students so that staff learns the neuro-scientific research that supports mindfulness for reducing stress, improving focus, and enhancing physical and Social Emotional Wellness.

✓ Start off staff meetings with a moment or two of mindfulness to model the importance, provide a shared experience, and to reduce stress/improve focus at the meetings.

✓ Encourage staff to use the "tardy bell" as a cue for taking one deep breath before class begins. As they inhale, they can say to themselves, "Breathing in, I do my best." As they exhale, they can say to themselves, "Breathing out, I let go of the rest."

SOCIAL EMOTIONAL WELLNESS MATTERS

"Well-being is fundamentally no different than learning to play the cello. If one practices the skills of well-being, one will get better at it."

- Richard Davidson (Davidson, R., 2016, para. 2)

Workplace stress is an issue that we must take seriously, as it has a detrimental impact on the process of teaching and learning as well as on the staff, students, and organization itself. Fortunately, it is a problem we can address. A positive school climate teamed with social support result in increased teacher satisfaction and motivation (Day et al., 2010) and decreased stress and burnout (Hakanen, et al., 2006; Leung & Lee, 2006). Organizations that actively create, support, and invest in opportunities to boost school climate strengthen the Social Emotional Wellness of their staff—a win-win for teachers, students, schools, districts, and communities.

The evidence is clear; well-being is the result of skills that can be learned and cultivated. As educational leaders prioritize a wellness culture and teachers choose to immerse themselves in it, students learn and practice the same social-emotional skills. Through this collective effort, we can cultivate a calmer, more compassionate climate in our schools.

References

Abry, T., Rimm-Kaufman, S. E., Larsen, R. A., & Brewer, A. J. (2013). The influence of fidelity of implementation on teacher–student interaction quality in the context of a randomized controlled trial of the responsive classroom approach. *Journal of School Psychology, 51*(4), 437-453.

American Federation of Teachers. (2015). *Quality of worklife survey.* Retrieved 12/17/15

http://www.aft.org/sites/default/files/worklifesurveyresults2015.pdf

Bishop, S. R., Lau, M., Shapiro, S., Carlson, L., Anderson, N. D., Carmody, J., et al.. (2004). Mindfulness: A proposed operational definition. *Clinical Psychology: Science and Practice, 11*(3), 230-241.

Brackett, M. A., Palomera, R., Mojsa-Kaja, J., Reyes, M. R., & Salovey, P. (2010). Emotion-regulation ability, burnout, and job satisfaction among british secondary-school teachers. *Psychology in the Schools, 47*(4), 406-417.

Brouwer, P., Brekelmans, M., Nieuwenhuis, L., & Simons, R. (2012). Fostering teacher community development: A review of design principles and a case study of an innovative interdisciplinary team. *Learning Environments Research, 15*(3), 319-344.

Byron, G., Ziedonis, D. M., McGrath, C., Frazier, J. A., deTorrijos, F., & Fulwiler, C. (2015; 2014). Implementation of mindfulness training for mental health staff: Organizational context and stakeholder perspectives. *Mindfulness, 6*(4), 861-872. doi:10.1007/s12671-014-0330-2

Cartwright, S., & Cooper, C. L. (2009). *The oxford handbook of organizational well-being* Oxford University Press, USA.

Cheng, L. P., & Ko, H. (2009). Teacher-team development in a school-based professional development program. *The Mathematics Educator, 19*(1)

Datnow, A. (2011). Collaboration and contrived collegiality: Revisiting hargreaves in the age of accountability. *Journal of Educational Change, 12*(2), 147-158.

Davidson, R. (March 21, 2016). The Four Keys to Well Being. Retrieved on January 5, 2017 from

http://greatergood.berkeley.edu/article/item/the_four_keys_to_well_being

Davidson, T. (May 27, 2011). Revealed: Teaching days lost to stress. *Hull Daily Mail,* pp. 1. Retrieved from

http://search.proquest.com.libproxy2.usc.edu/docview/869120462?accounti d=14749

Day, C., Sammons, P., & Stobart, G. (2007). *Teachers matter: Connecting work, lives and effectiveness* McGraw-Hill Education (UK).

Erogul, M., Singer, G., McIntyre, T., & Stefanov, D. G. (2014). Abridged mindfulness intervention to support wellness in first-year medical students. *Teaching and Learning in Medicine, 26*(4), 350-356. doi:10.1080/10401334.2014.945025

Flook, L., Goldberg, S. B., Pinger, L., & Davidson, R. J. (2015). Promoting prosocial behavior and self-regulatory skills in preschool children through a mindfulness-based kindness curriculum. *Developmental Psychology, 51*(1), 44.

Flook, L., Goldberg, S. B., Pinger, L., Bonus, K., & Davidson, R. J. (2013). Mindfulness for teachers: A pilot study to assess effects on stress, burnout, and teaching efficacy. *Mind, Brain, and Education, 7*(3), 182-195. doi:10.1111/mbe.12026

Fries, M. (2009). Mindfulness based stress reduction for the changing work environment. *Journal of Academic and Business Ethics, 2*, 1-10. Retrieved from http://search.proquest.com.libproxy1.usc.edu/docview/759646647?accounti d=14749

Gallup. (March 28, 2013). *U.S. teachers love their lives, but struggle in the workplace.* Retrieved 12/17, 2015, from http://www.gallup.com/poll/161516/teachers-love-lives-struggle-workplace.aspx

Gelles, D. (2015). Mindful work: How meditation is changing business from the inside out Houghton Mifflin Harcourt.

Goleman, D. (2006). The Socially Intelligent Leader. *Teaching to Student Strengths.* 64(1), 76-81, Retrieved January 5, 2017 from http://www.ascd.org/publications/educational-leadership/sept06/vol64/num01/The-Socially-Intelligent-Leader.aspx.

Green, G. R. (2014). Study to investigate self-reported teacher absenteeism and desire to leave teaching as they relate to teacher-reported teaching satisfaction, job-related stress, symptoms of depression, irrational beliefs, and self- efficacy. (Ph.D., City University of New York). *ProQuest Dissertations and Theses,* Retrieved from http://search.proquest.com.libproxy1.usc.edu/docview/1566949089?account id=14749

Hakanen, J. J., Bakker, A. B., & Schaufeli, W. B. (2006). Burnout and work engagement among teachers. *Journal of School Psychology, 43*(6), 495-513.

Heaphy, E. D., & Dutton, J. E. (2008). Positive social interactions and the human body at work: Linking organizations and physiology. *Academy of Management Review, 33*(1), 137-162.

House, J. S., Landis, K. R., & Umberson, D. (1988). Social relationships and health. *Science (New York, N.Y.), 241*(4865), 540-545.

Hunter, J. (2013). Is mindfulness good for business? *Mindful Magazine,* , 52-59.

Hydon, S., Wong, M., Langley, A. K., Stein, B. D., & Kataoka, S. H. (2015). Preventing secondary traumatic stress in educators. *Child and Adolescent Psychiatric Clinics of North America, 24*(2), 319-333.

Jennings, P. A., Frank, J. L., Snowberg, K. E., Coccia, M. A., & Greenberg, M. T. (2013). Improving classroom learning environments by cultivating awareness and resilience in education (CARE): Results of a randomized controlled trial. *School Psychology Quarterly, 28*(4), 374.

Kabat-Zinn, J. (2003). Mindfulness-based interventions in context: Past, present, and future. *Clinical Psychology: Science and Practice, 10*(2), 144. Retrieved from http://usc.summon.serialssolutions.com

Kendziora, K., & Yoder, N. (2016). When districts support and integrate social and emotional learning (SEL).

Lee, R. M., Draper, M., & Lee, S. (2001). Social connectedness, dysfunctional interpersonal behaviors, and psychological distress: Testing a mediator model. *Journal of Counseling Psychology, 48*(3), 310.

Leung, D. Y., & Lee, W. W. (2006). Predicting intention to quit among chinese teachers: Differential predictability of the components of burnout. *Anxiety, Stress, and Coping, 19*(2), 129-141.

Morledge, T. J., Allexandre, D., Fox, E., Fu, A. Z., Higashi, M. K., Kruzikas, D. T., et al.. (2013). Feasibility of an online mindfulness program for stress Management—A randomized, controlled trial. *Annals of Behavioral Medicine, 46*(2), 137-148. doi:10.1007/s12160-013-9490-x

Oberle, E., & Schonert-Reichl, K. A. (2016). Stress contagion in the classroom? the link between classroom teacher burnout and morning cortisol in elementary school students. *Social Science & Medicine, 159*, 30-37.

Ozaki, K., Motohashi, Y., Kaneko, Y., & Fujita, K. (2012). Association between psychological distress and a sense of contribution to society in the workplace. *BMC Public Health, 12*(1), 1.

Plauborg, H. (2009). Opportunities and limitations for learning within teachers' collaboration in teams: Perspectives from action learning. *Action Learning: Research and Practice, 6*(1), 25-34.

Pressman, S.D., Cohen, S., Miller, G.E., Barken, A., Rabin, S., & Treanor, J.J. (2005). Loneliness, social network size, and immune response to influenza vaccination in college freshmen. *Health Psychology, 24*(3), 297-305, Retrieved December 29, 2016 from http://www.psy.cmu.edu/~scohen/Pressman%20et%20al%20HP2005.pdf

"Quotes – Empathy Circles (n.d.)." Retrieved January 5, 2017 fromhttp://cultureofempathy.com/references/Quotes/Empathy-Circles.htm.

Ransford, C. R., Greenberg, M. T., Domitrovich, C. E., Small, M., & Jacobson, L. (2009). The role of teachers' psychological experiences and perceptions of curriculum supports on the implementation of a social and emotional learning curriculum. *School Psychology Review, 38*(4), 510.

Ross, S. W., Romer, N., & Horner, R. H. (2011). Teacher well-being and the implementation of schoolwide positive behavior interventions and supports.
Journal of Positive Behavior Interventions, , 1098300711413820.

Skaalvik, E. M., & Skaalvik, S. (2015). Job satisfaction, stress and coping strategies
in the teaching profession-what do teachers say? *International Education Studies*,
8(3), 181-192. Retrieved from
http://search.proquest.com.libproxy2.usc.edu/docview/1667047535?account
id=14749

Stevenson, A., & Harper, S. (2006). Workplace stress and the student learning experience. *Quality Assurance in Education, 14*(2), 167-178.

Taylor, C., Harrison, J., Haimovitz, K., Oberle, E., Thomson, K., Schonert-Reichl,
K., et al.. (2016). Examining ways that a mindfulness-based intervention re-
duces stress in public school teachers: A mixed-methods study. *Mindfulness*,
7(1), 115-129. doi:10.1007/s12671-015-0425-4

Teachers Assurance Report. (2013). *High stress levels are taking their toll within the teaching profession*. Retrieved 12/17, 2015, from
http://s3.documentcloud.org/documents/725354/teachers-assurance-stress-
research-infographic.pdf

"Viktor E. Frankl (n.d.)." BrainyQuote.com. Retrieved January 4, 2017 from
https://www.brainyquote.com/quotes/quotes/v/viktorefr160380.html

Visscher, A., & Witziers, B. (2004). Subject departments as professional communities? *British Educational Research Journal, 30*(6), 785-800.

Yu, X., Wang, P., Zhai, X., Dai, H., & Yang, Q. (2015). The effect of work stress
on job burnout among teachers: The mediating role of self-efficacy. *Social Indicators Research, 122*(3), 701-70.

CHAPTER 7

Repair, Restore, and Build Resilience In An Intervention Room Setting

Debra Sacks and Jessie Fuller

Student attendance and engagement are critical for student outcomes. Students who continue to cause classroom disruptions or engage in undesired behavior on campus require intensive interventions designed to improve social-emotional skill development and restore the community.

"Today, many schools are rightfully concerned about the numbers of all types of students who are being suspended or expelled for their behavior" (Skiba et al., 2002). A significant concern is that the greatest number includes minority students who are suspended and expelled more often and for longer periods for the same infractions than their white counterparts.

Punitive consequence seldom changes student behavior or deter others from engaging in similar practices (Skiba et al., 1999, 1997). Contrary to the discipline intention or assumption of changing behavior, the suspended student experiences a more difficult academic path, thus increasing the likelihood of dropping out and facing additional adverse life outcomes.

Many schools are now examining and revising site and district policies in an attempt to rely less on exclusionary consequences that

> ### Questions Regarding Universal Practices:
>
> ☐ Are all the tenants of PBIS Tier I in place?
> ☐ Are community-building circles practiced to build social capital and increase student Social Emotional Learning (SEL) skills?
> ☐ Does the staff review data to find correlations in behavior and student academic success?
> ☐ Are we intentional about developing relationships, asking reflective questions, and providing opportunities to restore relationships (with school staff, peers, and family)?
> ☐ Do we teach resiliency skills?

push students out of education and into the juvenile justice system. Schools working to improve their current discipline system and response to student behavior can start by asking essential questions about their universal practices and disciplinary approach.

The lists on this page and page 53 include questions regarding both universal practices and discipline policies. Consideration of each factor can assist the school team in becoming more restorative and responsive in their approach to correcting behavior.

The Resiliency Room Model

It is important for schools to find creative ways to address challenging behaviors in non-exclusionary ways that decrease repeat behavior. Providing a space for students to learn and develop social-emotional competencies is essential. One example is the Resiliency Room Model. Core to this model is the development of resilience.

Resilience, or the ability to bounce back from a setback, refers to the process of adapting to adversity. Adverse experiences can include traumatic events, tragedy, or significant environmental stressors (i.e. family problems, financial issues, and major health concerns).

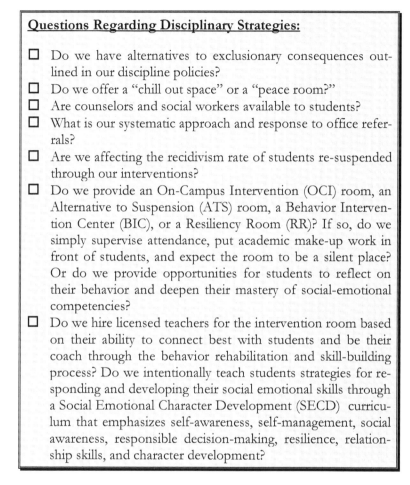

<u>Questions Regarding Disciplinary Strategies:</u>

☐ Do we have alternatives to exclusionary consequences outlined in our discipline policies?

☐ Do we offer a "chill out space" or a "peace room?"

☐ Are counselors and social workers available to students?

☐ What is our systematic approach and response to office referrals?

☐ Are we affecting the recidivism rate of students re-suspended through our interventions?

☐ Do we provide an On-Campus Intervention (OCI) room, an Alternative to Suspension (ATS) room, a Behavior Intervention Center (BIC), or a Resiliency Room (RR)? If so, do we simply supervise attendance, put academic make-up work in front of students, and expect the room to be a silent place? Or do we provide opportunities for students to reflect on their behavior and deepen their mastery of social-emotional competencies?

☐ Do we hire licensed teachers for the intervention room based on their ability to connect best with students and be their coach through the behavior rehabilitation and skill-building process? Do we intentionally teach students strategies for responding and developing their social emotional skills through a Social Emotional Character Development (SECD) curriculum that emphasizes self-awareness, self-management, social awareness, responsible decision-making, resilience, relationship skills, and character development?

Researchers have found several factors that contribute to a person's resiliency, including supportive relationships, emotional management, and personal mastery. Of these, caring and supportive relationships both within and outside of the family unit are considered an essential feature to the development of resiliency (American Psychological Association, 2016). The list on page 54 includes additional skills required for the development of resiliency.

The aim of the Resiliency Room (RR) is for the adult in the room to do things *with* students and to increase the likelihood of

Elements of Resiliency according to the American Psychological Association (2016) include:

✓ Feeling in control of one's life
✓ Knowing how to develop stress hardiness
✓ Being empathic
✓ Possessing effective communication and interpersonal skills,
✓ Having sound problem solving and decision-making skills
✓ Setting realistic goals and expectations
✓ Learning from success and failure
✓ Being a compassionate and contributing member of society
✓ Living a responsible life
✓ Feeling special and helping others to feel the same

seeing a change in behavior and decreasing behavior recidivism. By utilizing the concept of Fair Process (Kim & Mauborgne, 1997), the teacher works with students to help them reflect on their behavior and listen to their viewpoint, while still upholding a clear expectation of what the student needs to do in the future to be successful. This practice is known as being in the "with box," according to the Restorative Practices Social Discipline Window (Costello et al., 2009). This process, led by a caring adult, builds resiliency into the climate of the room, often changing outcomes.

In one example, a California high school implemented the Resiliency Room (RR) model at the start of the 2016-17 school year. Recent data indicated that 1 of 75 students returned to the RR for a new behavior infraction during the first semester. In individual interviews with students in the RR, one student described the process as different from anything he had ever experienced after repeated suspensions since 7th grade. He stated that the RR teacher appeared to "really care." Her interactions with the student were respectful, fair and non-judgmental. Another student admitted that he no longer wanted to put himself and his parents through "this." He explained how he plans to use the skills he has learned in the modules, like engaging in breathing exercises instead of letting his monkey brain (firing amygdala) take over.

Fair Process

As stated earlier, an essential element within the Resiliency Room model is the restorative approach of Fair Process. This concept advocates doing things "with" people as opposed to "to" people. This applies both to reactive situations (i.e. crisis management) and proactive strategies. Authors of the concept state that "…Individuals are most likely to trust and cooperate freely with systems—whether they themselves win or lose by those systems—when fair process is observed" ("Defining Restorative: 4.6 Fair Process," n.d., para. 1).

The Three Principles of Fair Process as stated in the Restorative Practices Handbook, International Institute for Restorative Practices (2009) include:

- *Engagement*—involve individuals in decision-making by listening to their views and genuinely taking their opinions into account
- *Explanation*—explain the rationale behind a decision to all stakeholders
- *Expectation Clarity*—make sure that everyone clearly understands decisions and resultant expectations

Community Circles

Another essential element of the Resiliency Model is Community Circles. Held each morning within the room, the teacher/coach facilitates the circles to build social capital, develop relationships, and restore student engagement and participation in the educational setting. The teacher works with students to develop a set of norms for the circle that includes bringing their best self to the circle, honoring other students' differences, honoring silence, being mindful, respecting confidentiality, and intending kindness and honesty. The talking piece is introduced as a tangible object that is passed to the person who agrees to talk next while others honor their contributions without interruption or response.

According to Lewis (2002), "Everything in the circle is an invitation. When you have the talking piece you are invited to speak, but you may pass. When you do not have the talking piece you are invited to listen."

Reflect and Relate

Another key element to creating a culture of resilience involves the initial introduction of the student(s) to the intervention. Called *Reflect and Relate*, the purpose of this component is to connect the teacher/coach to the student(s) and the intention of the Resiliency Room intervention. Typically accomplished through a circle (if the group is large) or a one-on-one meeting, the teacher explains the goal of the Resiliency Room and provides a personal introduction, including the desire to help students in the RR improve their social and academic success. After being part of the Community Circle, students work independently, reflecting on a series of questions related to the incident(s) that lead up to participation in the Resiliency Room. The student completes the questions on his or her first day of attendance.

Informal Pre-Conference:

The teacher/coach conducts an informal pre-conference with the student to orally share the student's responses to the Reflect and Relate questions. The pre-conference provides an opportunity for the student to share individual perspectives and further develop the relationship with the significant adult(s) in the room.

Social-Emotional Curriculum Modules:

A major focus of the RR model is the development of the students' social-emotional skills. This is accomplished through specific modules that address behavior-specific skill areas. Each module requires a student to complete a character strengths survey, a growth mindset assignment, a mindfulness exercise as well as behavior-specific assignments designed to increase pro-social attitudes and behaviors, and decrease maladaptive behaviors.

Modules include videos, articles, surveys, and activities that promote students' social and emotional learning, character development, and personal reflection. Strategies to increase impulse control, empathy, kindness, gratitude, forgiveness, happiness, self-awareness, social awareness, relationship skills, self-management, and responsible decision-making are also included within the lessons.

Module assignments are presented and discussed with the teacher/coach. The teacher/coach of record maintains the individual student data and submitted assignments.

Restore and/or Repair:

Once a student completes a module, he or she will be required to answer questions related to self and social restoration. These questions enable the student to further develop social-emotional competencies.

The final stage in the Resiliency Room intervention process is for the student to identify an adult ally on campus to help the student maintain positive behavior, thus impacting the student's educational success. The ally may be a teacher, campus security officer, campus supervisor, librarian, secretary, counselor, instructional aide, attendance clerk, athletic coach, etc. and serves as a mentor to the student.

The Resiliency Room and similar "alternative to suspension" models are designed to change student behavior by increasing the core competencies that enable appropriate behavior. By shifting the focus to skill development, students have the opportunity to master their ability to manage their emotional reactions and schools are able to more permanently reduce disciplinary concerns.

For more information about the Resiliency Room Model, contact a CLS representative at https://www.clsteam.net/contact/ or call 888-297-6096.

References

American Psychological Association. (December 2016). Washington, DC. Retrieved December 20, 2016 from http://www.apa.org/helpcenter/road-resilience.aspx

Costello, B., Wachtel, J., Wachtel, J. (2009). The Restorative Practices Handbook.

"Defining Restorative: 4.6 Fair Process." Retrieved January 20, 2016 from http://www.iirp.edu/what-we-do/what-is-restorative-practices/defining-restorative/18-fair-process

Kim, Wl, & Mauborgne, R. (1997). Fair Process. Harvard Business Review, January 1.

Lewis, G. (2002). "Dreaming of a new reality," The Third International Conference on Conferencing, Circles and Other Restorative Practices, August 8-10, 2002, Minneapolis, Minnesota.

Skiba, R., Michael, R., Nardo, A., & Peterson, R.L. (December, 2002). The color of discipline: Sources of racial and gender disproportionality in school punishment. *The Urban Review, 34*(4), 317-342.

Skiba R.J., Peterson, R.L. & Williams, T. (January, 1999). The dark side of zero tolerance: Can punishment lead to safe schools? *Phi Delta Kappan, 80*(5), 372-381.

Skiba R.J., Peterson, R.L. & Williams, T. (August, 1997). Office referrals and suspension: Disciplinary intervention in middle schools. *Education and Treatment of Children, 20*(3), 1-21.

CHAPTER 8

Building a Positive School Climate Through Mental Health Support

Christine Fonseca

Every Monday throughout the school year thousands of students and educators head back to the classroom. Some are excited and hopeful. Some are ambivalent or apathetic. And some are terrified. Impacted by a variety of mental health challenges, many of the students in our education system arrive at school ill-equipped to handle the stressors they will face. The result: behavioral problems as some students externalize their frustration and anger. Those who don't show outward manifestations of their stress will often turn inward, developing intense stress and anxiety that can slowly eat away at their confidence and resilience.

Researchers estimate that as many as 63% of children experience one or more adverse childhood experiences, or ACEs, including neglect, abuse, and parental divorce. Upwards of 12% experience multiple ACEs resulting in significant levels of toxic stress that can negatively impact school functioning (Felitti, 1998). Further, recent statistics estimate that 1 in 5 school-aged children live with mild to moderate mental health challenges ("Mental Health in Schools," n.d., para. 1). Worse, 17% of children in grades 9 – 12 have suicidal ideations ("Suicide: Facts at a glance," 2015) and/or engage in self-harm behaviors. Suicide is the second leading cause of death for children and third for adolescents, accounting for more death than cancer, car accidents and other illnesses combined ("Facts and Stats," n.d).

Despite the significance of concern, many children do not receive care for their mental health needs. Barriers including an inability to pay for services, the negative stigma associated with mental illness and mental health challenges, and lack of awareness prevent children from treatment, often with worsening outcomes. When children don't obtain the necessary support for their mental health needs, leaving their problems undiagnosed and/or untreated, adverse consequences for learning and social-emotional development occur.

With all of the indicators of increased mental health concerns with children in the United States, it is not surprising that states have begun to legislate mandates for schools to support mental health and behavior. In California, recent legislation (AB2246) calls for a school-based suicide prevention policy that focuses on prevention, intervention and crisis management for all 7-12 grade students, especially those considered high risk (LGBTQ youth, foster youth, and others). Similar mandates exist throughout the United States, calling on schools to aid in supporting the mental health of our children through prevention, identification, intervention and crisis management (Kilgus, 2015).

Schools are in a unique position to help support the mental health needs of children. Creating systems that reduce the stigma of mental illness through awareness, support the development of social-emotional competencies, strengthen mental wellness, and link to community services when needed result in improvements in social and emotional functioning as well as improved academic outcomes (Stephan, 2013, slide 25).

A Tale of Two Structures

Researchers support the use of multi-tiered systems of support including MTSS and PBIS to address social behavior concerns, including aggression, oppositional behavior and attention concerns (Barnett, 2013). Common interventions under this model frame social behavioral concerns within an ecological-behavioral model, focusing on making changes within the environment in order to change student behavior. Universal supports focus on manipulating the environment through the establishment of expectations, systems of acknowledgment and correction, and the use of data to drive decision-making.

Despite the strengths of the ecological-behavioral model for use with externalizing behaviors, similar support for internalized behaviors, including anxiety and depression, is not found. These types of behavior are commonly supported through the use of a model that focuses on cognitive skill development and coping strategies (McIntosh, 2014). This model focuses less on environmental changes and more on changes within the individual. Decisions are based on data that relies more heavily on subjective data (i.e. behavior rating scales), and less on the types of data utilized in traditional MTSS and PBIS structures.

Current research focuses on braiding both models in order to provide a comprehensive approach to supporting the mental health needs of students. Herman et. al. (2004) described a multi-tiered depression prevention model in which psycho-social factors within the school setting were targeted as well as individual coping strategies in order to both teach and promote new, adaptive behaviors. Results of the study indicated better outcomes when both models were utilized. In another study, Cook et. al. (2015) combined PBIS universal supports (teaching and acknowledging expectations) with social-emotional learning (SEL) curriculum delivered to all students. Results indicated significant improvements to both externalizing and internalizing behavior compared to utilization of either strand individually. While additional research is needed across multiple grades, it's clear that combining a social-ecological approach with a cognitive skills approach yields the most promising results to support the mental wellness of students.

School-based mental health models, including the Interconnected Systems Framework (ISF), suggest utilizing a multi-tiered approach to promoting mental health. ISF advocates weaving school-based mental health structures into the existing multi-tiered system of MTSS or PBIS, with the additional focus on mental wellness at Tier I, specific skill development at Tier II, and highly specialized intervention and skill development at Tier III (Barnett, 2013; Stephan, 2013, slide 58).

Mental Health Support Across the Tiers

As school districts move toward including school-based mental health supports at the school sites, it is important to take stock of existing structures and programs, utilizing these as appropriate. Cultivating a strong commitment from district and site level administration is also imperative. Ensuring that all parties, from management to support staff, understand mental wellness and mental illness, including training in mental health first aid and the specific ways schools can address mental health needs is a vital component to any school-based mental health structure. Districts should focus on providing training for staff and building capacity as the first step toward implementing mental health support on school campuses.

The next sections outline specific structures needed at each of the tiers within a multi-tiered system.

Tier I – Universal Supports

Tier I provides proactive and preventative structures needed to support all children in the development of pro-social behavior and mental wellness. A focus on mental health awareness, along with strategies to remove the stigma associated with mental illness, as well as creating an inclusive school community will create a positive school climate. This, in turn, acts as a protection factor for students, providing the foundation needed for mental wellness.

The chart on page 64 indicates the evidenced-based best practices necessary to support social behavior and mental health of students. Incorporation of most to all of these structures is most likely to ensure access to support for all students, including those at highest risk for mental health concerns.

Tier II Supports – Targeted Interventions

Tier II focuses on targeted interventions for specific groups that have demonstrated a need for additional supports. In order to meet this need, districts and sides must determine the pathways students can use to access additional support. Structures that include a screening process and a way to ensure the fidelity of implementation of the evidence-based interventions are vital to the success of a Tier II structure. Furthermore, a process to evaluate the efficacy and fidelity of the screening and matching-need-to-intervention processes should be considered when developing a robust Tier II system to address social-emotional needs of students. As with Tier I, school-based teams for Tier II or III should include mental health personnel with knowledge of potential interventions and supports.

TIER I BEST PRACTICES:
UNIVERSAL SUPPORT FOR SOCIAL BEHAVIOR AND
MENTAL WELLNESS

➢ Include a mental health professional on a Tier I team to assist in the development of mental wellness awareness efforts

➢ Develop PBIS structures, including defining and teaching expectations for behavior, acknowledging appropriate behavior, and using data for problem-solving and decision-making

➢ Use a restorative process for correcting behavior, one that focuses on the development of lagging social-emotional skills

➢ Provide opportunities for students to develop and practice social-emotional learning competencies, including self-awareness, emotional self-management, and problem-solving

➢ Teach universal coping strategies to address anger, frustration, stress and anxiety

➢ Develop awareness and inclusion campaigns designed to reduce stigma associated with specific groups or diagnoses

The chart on the following page includes the best practices and considerations a district and/or site will need when developing the Tier II structure to address both the social-behavioral and mental health needs of the school.

Additional to the structural considerations, districts must identify service providers for interventions, as well as who will engage in progress monitoring and fidelity measures.

It is important to note that schools face a challenge in addressing the needs of students with internalizing behaviors. Most interventions demonstrate little to no significant positive impact to students (Kilgus, 2015). However recent research has indicated that combining well-known evidence-based interventions with cognitive-behavioral elements can address the needs of students with dealing with anxiety

---

**TIER II BEST PRACTICES:
TARGETED INTERVENTIONS FOR SOCIAL
BEHAVIOR AND MENTAL WELLNESS**

➤ Develop a process to screen and identify students in need of additional social behavioral or mental health support

➤ Use data to evaluate and connect a student's need to possible evidence-based interventions

➤ Provide evidence-based, targeted interventions that include increased instruction in cognitive skill areas (including problem-solving skills, executive functioning, and social emotional competencies), opportunities to practice skills outside of the intervention setting, and progress monitoring tools

➤ Determine and utilize fidelity measures to evaluate the identification of students, assessment of need, implementation of interventions, and results

---

and similar concerns. In one study, Dart et. al. (2015) utilized the popular intervention Check-In, Check-out (CICO), modifying it to include a peer-mediation component and cognitive-behavioral instruction. Although the study was small, initial research suggests that adapting and innovating current school-based interventions utilizing research can prove effective in meeting the needs of students with internalized behavior.

Tier III Supports – Intensive, Individualized Interventions

Some students require more significant interventions than those offered through universal support or Tier II. These students demonstrate intense needs and require interventions that are long-term, possibly requiring support that extends beyond the school setting. Districts committed to developing a school-based mental health model must consider how to help students who demonstrate such significant needs. Access to mental health services, either through the school district or the community, is paramount. Furthermore, support for the family will likely be required if students are going to make lasting progress.

Chapter 9, "Five Core Components of a Tier III Program for Students Exhibiting Challenging Behaviors," describes the components of a school-based program for Tier III students. In addition to the development of a full program to address Tier III needs, districts should develop a process to link student's need to community resources. Assigning specific district and site personnel to assist with the coordination of care and services is vital if districts are not only going to support the difficult challenges students at this level face but also maintain the student's access to the "least restrictive environment." The inclusion of the parents, including the availability of home visits and parenting training, is also essential to a Tier III system.

The chart on page 67 highlights a few of the best practices involved in developing a strong Tier III system of support.

To meet the legal mandates of AB 2246 and others, schools will need to develop ways to address post-crisis management ("AB2246 – Suicide Prevention In Schools, n.d., para. 3). Utilizing mental health professionals to coordinate a student's transition back to the school community is vital to the well-being of the entire community. This includes coordination of care with the student, the family, any community resources and the school community. Continued access to universal supports help the reintegration process.

> ## TIER III BEST PRACTICES: INTENSE AND INDIVIDUAL INTERVENTIONS FOR SOCIAL BEHAVIOR AND MENTAL WELLNESS
>
> ➢ Develop a process for linking to community services
>
> ➢ Assign district and site personnel for case management and coordination of care between service providers
>
> ➢ Offer support to both the student and the family
>
> ➢ Develop individualized plans to address both social-behavioral concerns (based on the function of behavior and development of replacement behaviors) and lagging skill development (based on psycho-social needs and the development of coping and cognitive skills)

What's Next?

The connection between mental health and academic performance is clear. As students' social-behavioral and emotional needs are supported, students are better able to learn. Grades, graduation rates, and school climate all improve when mental health support is offered universally for students (Geierstanger, 2004). But, simply providing a little mental awareness, some interventions and a referral list of community resources aren't enough. Genuine support requires a framework, a system that incorporates existing structures, develops a strong commitment at the district and site levels, and focuses on sustainability and implementation fidelity.

Yes, that sounds like a lot of work. Many of you may wonder how you are supposed to take on this task. Or even why you should.

Why wouldn't you?

The evidence is clear—supporting a student's mental health is vital. More than 5000 children attempt suicide every day in the United States ("Facts and Stats," n.d.). Too many of them are successful.

It's time to change this trajectory, to remove the stigma surrounding mental illness and build mental wellness into the fabric of our society, including our schools.

Our children deserve nothing less.

References

AB 2246 - Suicide Prevention Policies in Schools. (n.d.). Retrieved on January 6, 2017 from http://www.eqca.org/wp-content/uploads/AB2246.pdf

Barnett, S., Eber, L., % West, M. (2013). *Advancing education effectiveness: Interconnecting school mental health and school-wide positive behavior support.* Retrieved January 4, 2017 from https://www.pbis.org/common/cms/files/Current%20Topics/Final-Monograph.pdf

Cook, C. R., Frye, M., Slemrod, T., Lyon, A. R., Renshaw, T. L., & Zhang, Y. (2015). An integrated approach to universal prevention: Independent and combined effects of PBIS and SEL on youths' mental health. *School Psychology Quarterly, 30*(2), 116-183. http://dx.doi.org/10.1037/spq0000102

Dart, E. H., Furlow, C. M., Collins, T. A., Brewer, E., Gresham, F. M., and Chenier, K. H. (2015). Peer-mediated Check-In/Check-Out for students at-risk for internalizing disorders. School Psychology Quarterly, 30(2), 229-243. http://dx.doi.org/10.1037/spq0000092

Evans, R., & Hurrell, C. (2016). The role of schools in children and young people's self-harm and suicide: systematic review and meta-ethnography of qualitative research. *BMC Public Health, 16*, 401. http://doi.org/10.1186/s12889-016-3065-2

Facts and Stats. (n.d.) Retrieved on January 2, 2017 from http://jasonfoundation.com/youth-suicide/facts-stats/

Felitti, V. J., Anda, R. F., Nordenberg, D., Williamson, D. F., Spitz, A. M., Edward, V., Koss, M. P., Marks, J. S. (1998). Relationship of childhood abuse and household dysfunction to many of the leading causes of death in adults: The Adverse Childhood Experiences (ACE) Study. *American Journal of Preventive Medicine 14*(4), 245-258. http://dx.doi.org/10.1016/S0749-3797(98)00017-8

Geierstanger, S. P., Amaral, G., Mansour, M., & Walters, S. R. (2004). School-based health centers and academic performance: Research, challenges, and recommendations. *Journal of School Health, 74*(9), 347-352. Retrieved on January 10, 2017 from https://www.researchgate.net/profile/Sara_Geierstanger/publication/8075674_School-Based_Health_Centers_and_Academic_Performance_Research_Challenges_and_Recommendations/links/0c96053b6c18f6a3e3000000.pdf

Herman, K. C., Merrell, K., Reinke, W. M., & Tucker, C. M. (2004). The role of school psychology in preventing depression. *Psychology in the Schools, 41*(7), 763-775. http://dx.doi.org/10.1002/pits.20016

Kilgus, S. P., Reinke, W. M., and Jimerson, S. R. (2015). Understanding mental health intervention and assessment within a multi-tiered framework: Contemporary science, practice, and policy. *School Psychology Quarterly, 30*(2), 159-165. http://dx.doi.org/10.1037/spq0000118

McIntosh, K., Ty, S. V., & Miller, L. D. (2014). Effects of school-wide positive behavior interventions and supports on internalizing behaviors: Current evidence and future directions. *Journal of Positive Behavior Intervention, 16*(4), 209-218. http://dx.doi.org/10.1177/1098300713491980

Mental Health in Schools. (n.d.). Retrieved on January 2, 2017 from http://www.nami.org/Learn-More/Public-Policy/Mental-Health-in-Schools

Stephan, S. H. (2013). Expanding PBIS Capacity with School Mental Health [PowerPoint slides], Retrieved on January 5, 2017 from http://www.pbis.org/common/cms/files/pbisresources/FridayAMKeynote_Stephan.pdf

Suicide: Facts at a glance. (2015). Retrieved on January 2, 2017 from https://www.cdc.gov/violenceprevention/pdf/suicide-datasheet-a.pdf

Five Core Components of a Tier III Program for Students Exhibiting Challenging Behaviors

Kenny McCarthy

The goal of education for many is to prepare children to become engaged citizens in society. However, instead of learning specific thinking strategies that move students toward global engagement, students only learn how to navigate a system removed from the real world context. Cognitive-based programming was developed to intentionally move students toward long-term growth and increase cognitive skill development. As education in the United States continues its advancement toward being culturally responsive, developmentally appropriate, and more individualized, so should our programming for marginalized youth (Mohr et al., 2009). Cognitive-based interventions are suitable for all students, particularly those who demonstrate lagging skill, are identified as having a disability, and those impacted by trauma and/or mental illness.

When developing a Tier III intervention program for students previously served in restrictive settings, there are five recommended core components:

- ❖ Authentic relationship development
- ❖ Positively-stated expectations for behavior
- ❖ Collaborative Problem Solving
- ❖ Goal Setting
- ❖ Skill Development

Authentic Relationship Development:

The development of positive relationships between educator and students is well-known to be essential in any classroom. This is particularly important within Tier III programs. Positive, respectful relationships between staff and students is a key factor for student engagement. Additionally, positive interactions with committed, concerned educators and other adults are one of the reasons why students stay in school (Lehr et al., 2004). Students are more likely to show resilience, demonstrate positive mindset shifts, social skill improvements, social-emotional awareness, and increased problem-solving skills when committed to authentic relationships that break the traditional ideology of teacher-student relationships.

Positively-stated Expectations:

The next component of a successful Tier III program is the development of positively-stated expectations across various settings. Authentic relationships in school settings must have expectations to guide all participants. "Students with emotional/behavioral disorders were less likely to drop out if they…were in schools that maintained high expectations of special education students" (Lehr et al., 2004, p. 13) These expectations provide a common language and behavior definition for all program participants.

It is important to develop expectations across a wide variety of settings. Experiences in multiple venues offer students opportunities to successfully navigate their world and practice code-switching skills.

Settings can include typical school environments including class-rooms, recess areas, physical education, and school-based activities. Additional non-school environments include job interviews, field trips, restaurants, and other public facilities. Establishing expectations with students' in various settings brings forth challenging behaviors. Challenging behaviors are a symptom of lagging skill development. These skill deficits rise to the surface when adults believe "students do well if they can" ("The Paperwork," n.d.).

Collaborative Problem Solving:

Identification of a student's lagging skill development leads to the third core component of a Tier III program—effective problem-solving strategies. Originally developed by Harvard Medical School psychiatrists, Drs. Stuart Ablon and Ross Greene, Collaborative Problem Solving (CPS) is an excellent example of a particular prob-lem-solving strategy utilized within a Tier III program ("Our Collab-orative Problem Solving Approach, n.d."). Opportunities to confront challenging behaviors among the adults and students will arise be-cause of unmet expectations. Specific problem-solving steps provide the adults with guidance on how to collaborate with students. The problem-solving steps target all of the Social Emotional Learning (SEL) core competencies. Through cognitive modeling, students learn to reflect adult thinking and develop the highly sought after skills of *empathy* and *flexibility*.

Goal Setting:

The problem-solving process leads to our fourth component of goal setting. Consistent goal setting provides students with opportunities to develop healthy attributions. Students with lagging skills often struggle to see how their decisions affect outcomes in various areas of their lives. Goal-setting practices are an effective vehicle through which students experience successes and failures. Processing through these opportunities leads to improvements in self-efficacy and more adaptive attribution (i.e. internal locus of control and increased optimism).

Attributions, or the way in which students attribute causes for their behavior, could be further investigated through the principal of *growth mindset*. Students who attribute their failures to external and uncontrollable sources, including bad luck, likability, and other means out of their control reflect a fixed mindset. This type of mindset leads to disengagement and poor persistence on future tasks. Goal setting provides an avenue of intentional practice. Students learn how to view events within the context of their actions, to see the correlation between choices and outcomes. This process enables students to shift away from their fixed mindset to a healthier, growth mindset, setting the stage for academic risk taking and increased positive outcomes (Dweck, 2008).

Skill Development:

The final component is the development of lagging cognitive skills, including executive functioning skills, problem-solving, and social-emotional competencies. Targeted skill development for each student is determined based upon specific inventories completed by educators and parents, as well as behavioral observations. SEL, Restorative Practices, PBIS, Growth-Mindset, tiered interventions and executive functioning skills are braided into the overall program design.

One option for embedding these practices into a comprehensive program is to develop a SEL calendar for the year, with a specific focus on each week. Staff wraps the specific skill into every part of the school day for the week, creating intentional opportunities for practice. Additionally, comprehensive programs should utilize proactive, restorative practices as a way to practice problem-solving strategies and build cognitive competencies.

Cognitive skills are most malleable during childhood. Development of these skills is a slow process, often with results that are not immediately observed. This runs counter to the majority of school-based Tier III programs which seek short-term gains as measured by a reduction of problem behaviors and increased compliance to school norms. Cognitive based programs focus more on long-term results, seeking to develop the skills necessary to move student toward successful adulthood.

It is important for schools to shift from short-term measures of success through behavior reduction, to goals that include increased use of social-emotional and cognitive competencies. Through my experience in developing Tier III programs, I have found these components of a cognitive-based model to be most effective in developing the thinking skills students need to lead productive lives.

References

Dweck, C. (2008). Mindset: The New Psychology Of Success. New York, NY : Ballantine Books.

Lehr, C., Johnson, D., Bremer, C., Cosio, A., & Thompson, M., (2004). "Increasing Rates of School Completion: Moving from Policy and Research to Practice." Retrieved on January 4, 2017 from
http://www.ncset.org/publications/essentialtools/dropout/

Mohr, W., Olson, J., Branca, N.,, Martin, A., & Pumariega, M.,(2009). "Beyond Points and Level Systems: Moving Toward Child-Centered Programming." *American Journal of Orthopsychiatry, 79*(1). 8-18. DOI: 10.1037/a0015375

"The Paperwork n.d." Retrieved on January 5, 2017 from
www.livesinthebalance.org/paperwork

"Our Collaborative Problem Solving Approach, n.d." Retrieved on January 5, 2017 from http://www.thinkkids.org/learn/our-collaborative-problem-solving-approach/

CHAPTER 10

Final Thoughts

Gail Angus

As you move forward and support the development of a positive school climate on your campuses and in your districts, don't forget the powerful messages and perspectives the authors shared with you. Individually, the articles compelled us to explore how our personal life experiences, our stories, influence our world view. To question how our experiences vary from person to person, students to students. Race, social-economic status, religion, and sexual preference influence our language and actions, often on an unconscious level. The words challenged us to take a risk and intentionally increase our awareness of *othering*. We were challenged to ask ourselves difficult questions. Do we only speak about the world from our individual perspectives? Or do we walk in another's shoes? Maybe we even allow others to be in their *own* shoes?

School climate transformation takes more than just being aware of your individual thoughts. It takes strong leaders who have the skills and knowledge to lead the transformation. The District and Site-Level Checklists provide guidance to ensure that any initiative will sustain over time. The social-emotional activities support building caring environments and foster healthy relationships for both students and staff. The Resiliency Room and Tier 3 programs share ways to include interventions which positively impact student behavior as well as the culture and climate of a school. Incorporating school-based mental health initiatives within a multi-tiered system further equip students, especially those at risk for poor mental health outcomes, to develop the social-emotional competencies necessary to be successful at school and in all aspects of their lives.

Youth face an increasingly violent and uncertain future. It is imperative that schools take an active role in disrupting this trajectory. Start with one suggestion or strategy presented in this book. Change how you interact with students and staff. Train staff to recognize mental health needs or increase their personal social-emotional competencies. Build interventions and programs to support high-risk students. No matter how you choose to begin, take action.

Creating a positive school climate is not easy. The work is messy and time consuming. You may wonder if the effort is worth it. I assure you, there is nothing more important. Each opportunity to positively impact the world of our students and schools is an opportunity to make a positive difference. Create a positive impact.

Transform your school culture.
Model change.
Be relentless.

Collaborative Learning Solutions – Collaborative Learning Solutions (CLS) partners with education agencies to provide innovative solutions addressing social-emotional wellness of students and staff.

Gail Angus, EdD - Gail Angus has more than 20 years of experience in public education as a teacher and administrator. She has been instrumental in leading large-scale system implementations involving multi-tier system of supports. Dr. Angus is one of the primary designers of the Education Monitoring Team (EMT) model, a framework for addressing Tier 2 and 3 needs of students. Currently, Dr. Angus is the Executive Director for CLS.

Jon Eyler, EdD – Jon Eyler is a national consultant and speaker on topics of educational psychology and equity. He works with executive leadership to implement cohesive systems of support and lead adaptive change around perception and mindset. He has taught and held various leadership positions in K-12 education. Additionally, he has taught courses in educational psychology at the University of Southern California (USC) in Los Angeles. Today, Dr. Eyler is the CEO of CLS, a national educational services and consulting firm based in Southern California.

Christine Fonseca, MS - Trained as a school psychologist, Christine Fonseca is an award-winning author, national speaker and consultant with CLS. She brings over 20 years of experience working with students and parents to her many articles and books. Critically acclaimed titles include *Emotional Intensity in Gifted Students: Helping Kids Cope with Explosive Feelings*, *Raising the Shy Child: A Parent's Guide to Social Anxiety*, and *I'm Not Just Gifted: Social-Emotional Curriculum for Guiding Gifted Children*.

Joelle Hood, MA - As a former "Teacher of the Year" and "Principal of the Year," Joelle brings over 20 years of experience, energy and passion to helping all educators thrive. She provides leadership coaching and professional learning to agencies across the nation, specializing in SEL, School Climate, Mindfulness, and Social Emotional Wellness/Resiliency for Educators.

Mary Beth Kropp, MA - Mary Beth Kropp has more than 30 years of experience in education as a teacher and site administrator. She currently works as a Senior Consultant with CLS, providing consultative and coaching services to educational agencies. Mary Beth holds an MA in Educational Leadership and is a doctoral student in Organizational Change and Leadership at the University of Southern California (USC) in Los Angeles.

Kenny McCarthy, MA - Kenny McCarthy is the Director of Programs for CLS. He provides consultation services for various Tier III programs throughout California, delivering individual coaching and professional learning targeted for classroom staff. He has previously served as a special education teacher using a cognitive-based program model.

Debra Sacks, EdD – Debra Sacks is a senior consultant with CLS. An educator for over 35 years, she has a passion for improving the lives of at-risk youth by providing professional learning experiences for adults and resources and strategies for youth. Dr. Sacks has developed SEL on-line courses for student interventions and trains in Restorative Practices, Mindfulness, SEL, and PBIS.

Micki Singer, JD - Micki has over 25 years of experience as a trial lawyer, teacher leader, and program director. She specializes in MTSS implementation and is the creator of the Student Justice Center, an innovative peer operated intervention system aimed at promoting equity through the use of restorative justice in the discipline process. Currently, Micki works as a senior consultant with CLS, providing consultation, professional learning, and coaching to education agencies.

Jessie Fuller, MA – As a former California League of School's Teacher of the Year with experience in both comprehensive and alternative settings, Jessie Fuller brings passion, knowledge and experience in SEL, resiliency, trauma-informed practices, and engagement to her work. She finds purpose in empowering both students and fellow educators, which she utilized in the co-creation of the Resiliency Room, an intervention model utilized in High Schools across California.

Pauline Stahl, Ed.D. – Pauline Stahl specializes in school-wide system change through state-of-the-art program design and reconceptualizing curriculum to increase access for all students. Dr. Stahl currently serves as the director and instructor of a dual enrollment genomics research program she developed for underrepresented high school students.

·

Made in the USA
Lexington, KY
03 May 2017